SPINOSAURUS

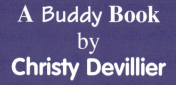

A Buddy Book
by
Christy Devillier

ABDO
Publishing Company

VISIT US AT

www.abdopub.com

Published by ABDO Publishing Company, 4940 Viking Drive, Edina, Minnesota 55435. Copyright © 2004 by Abdo Consulting Group, Inc. International copyrights reserved in all countries. No part of this book may be reproduced in any form without written permission from the publisher.

Printed in the United States.

Edited by: Michael P. Goecke
Contributing Editor: Matt Ray
Graphic Design: Denise Esner, Maria Hosley
Image Research: Deborah Coldiron
Illustrations: Deborah Coldiron, Maria Hosley
Photographs: Corbis, Corel, Digital Stock, Imagelibrary, Minden Pictures, Photodisc

Library of Congress Cataloging-in-Publication Data

Devillier, Christy, 1971-
    Spinosaurus/Christy Devillier.
        p. cm.
    Includes index.
    Summary: Describes the physical characteristics, habitat, and behavior of a big, meat-eating dinosaur that is famous for the tall spines along its back.
    ISBN 1-59197-539-5
    1. Spinosaurus—Juvenile literature. [1. Spinosaurus. 2. Dinosaurs.] I. Title.

QE862.S3D48 2004
567.912—dc22

                                                                        2003057811

TABLE OF CONTENTS

The Spinosaurus was a big, meat-eating dinosaur. It lived about 95 million years ago. The Spinosaurus is famous for the tall spines on its back.

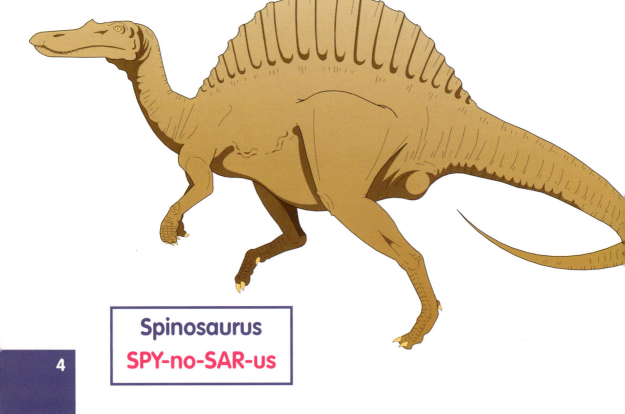

Spinosaurus
SPY-no-SAR-us

4

The Spinosaurus may have been about 50 feet (15 m) long. That is longer than a school bus.

Some scientists believe the Spinosaurus weighed as much as 16,000 pounds (7,300 kg). This is heavier than an elephant.

The Spinosaurus was heavier than an elephant.

 OW DID THEY MOVE?

The Spinosaurus walked on its two back legs. It may have used its arms for walking, too. The Spinosaurus's arms were smaller than its legs. It had three fingers on each hand. The Spinosaurus had a long tail, too.

TAIL

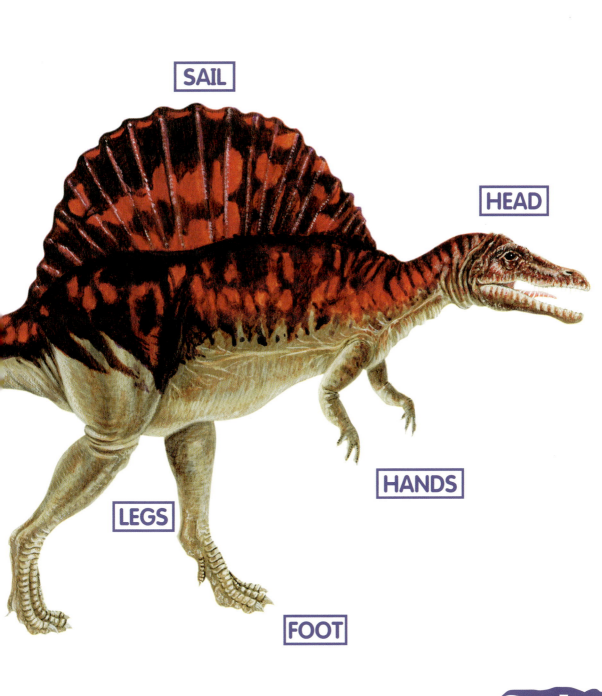

SAIL

HEAD

HANDS

LEGS

FOOT

7

WHY WERE THEY SPECIAL?

The Spinosaurus's name means "spiny lizard." Scientists named the Spinosaurus after the long spines on its back. Some of its spines were six feet (two m) long.

Scientists believe the spines were covered with skin. They think the skin-covered spines formed a "sail." Other dinosaurs have sails. But the Spinosaurus's sail may have been the tallest.

Six Feet (two m)

Some of the Spinosaurus's spines were as tall as a person.

What did the Spinosaurus use its sail for? Maybe sunshine on the sail helped it get warm. Wind blowing on the Spinosaurus's sail may have helped it cool down. Maybe the Spinosaurus used its sail to attract mates, too.

The Spinosaurus lived in northern Africa. It was around during the Cretaceous period. Back then, the continents were in different places. Africa was closer to South America.

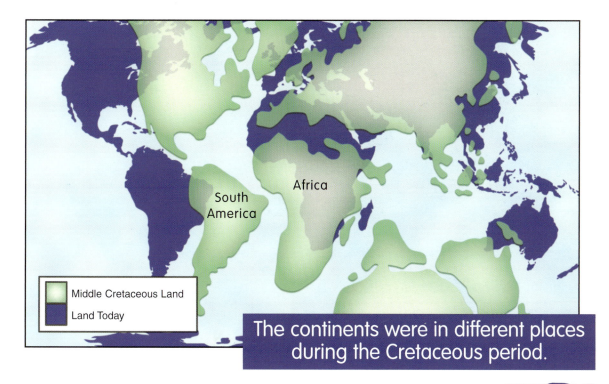

South America

Africa

Middle Cretaceous Land

Land Today

The continents were in different places during the Cretaceous period.

Today the Sahara desert covers northern Africa. This land was much different during the Cretaceous period. Back then, the weather was tropical. There were many forests. Some scientists believe the Spinosaurus lived near water.

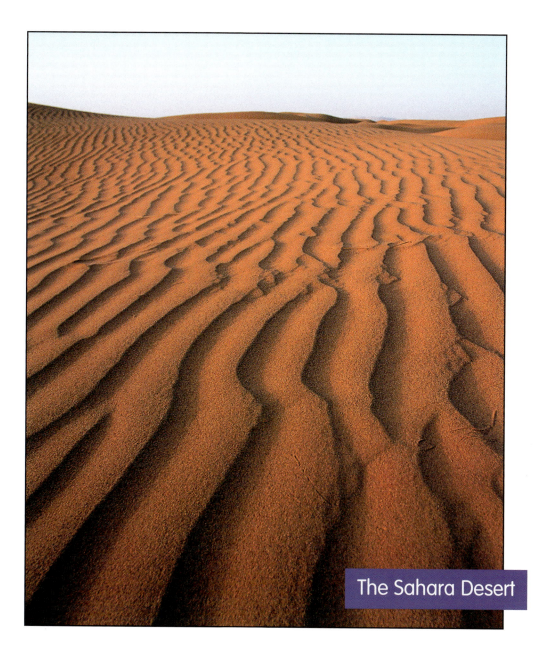

The Sahara Desert

13

WHO ELSE LIVED THERE?

The Spinosaurus lived among other animals. There were insects, such as ants, butterflies, and grasshoppers. Mammals lived in the forests. Birds and pterosaurs flew in the skies. Pterosaurs are flying reptiles.

The Spinosaurus lived among
many kinds of insects.

Many kinds of animals lived in the oceans. There were giant turtles, fish, and ammonites. Ammonites lived inside a shell. They ate other sea animals. Some ammonites were as small as a coin. The biggest ones were about three feet (one m) wide. Ammonites died out about 65 million years ago.

An ammonite fossil

17

The Spinosaurus lived among other dinosaurs, too. One was the Ouranosaurus. Like the Spinosaurus, the Ouranosaurus had a sail on its back.

The Ouranosaurus was a big dinosaur. It was about 24 feet (seven m) long. The Ouranosaurus ate plants with a toothless beak.

The Ouranosaurus had a toothless beak.

The Spinosaurus had a long mouth full of teeth.

The Spinosaurus was a carnivore. Carnivores eat meat. The Spinosaurus hunted and ate animals.

19

The Spinosaurus had a long mouth like a crocodile. Its teeth were long and cone-shaped. Some scientists believe the Spinosaurus also ate fish.

The Spinosaurus may also have killed and eaten other dinosaurs. Maybe the Spinosaurus scavenged for food, too. Scavengers eat animals they did not kill.

The Spinosaurus belongs to the Spinosauridae family. All the spinosaur dinosaurs were meat eaters. They had a long mouth like a crocodile.

A crocodile's long mouth.

21

Another spinosaur was the Baryonyx. The Baryonyx was smaller than the Spinosaurus. It was about 32 feet (10 m) long.

The Baryonyx's name means "heavy claw." This dinosaur had a very long claw on each hand. This claw was about 12 inches (30 cm) long.

The Baryonyx's long mouth was full of sharp teeth. Scientists believe it ate fish.

The Baryonyx had sharp teeth (above) and claws (below).

23

DISCOVERY

Paleontologists study fossils. This is how they learn about dinosaurs. A German paleontologist found the first Spinosaurus fossils. His name was Ernst von Stromer.

Paleontologists study fossils such as this one to learn about dinosaurs.

In 1912, Stromer found many Spinosaurus bones in Egypt. The bones almost formed a complete skeleton. A museum in Germany displayed the Spinosaurus fossils. But these fossils are not around today. They were destroyed years ago during World War II.

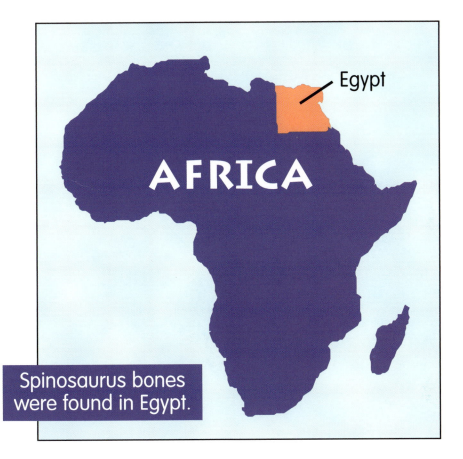

Egypt

AFRICA

Spinosaurus bones were found in Egypt.

There are very few Spinosaurus bones around today. Scientists hope to find more fossils in Africa. They want to learn more about this exciting dinosaur.

WHERE ARE THEY TODAY?

The Canadian Museum of Nature
Victoria Memorial Museum Building
240 McLeod Street (at Metcalfe Street)
Ottawa, Ontario, Canada
http://nature.ca/nature_e.cfm

GEAL - Museu da Lourinha
Morada: Rua Joao Luis de Moura,
2530 Lourinha, Portugal

SPINOSAURUS

NAME MEANS	Spiny Lizard
DIET	Meat
WEIGHT	Up to 16,000 pounds (7,300 kg)
LENGTH	50 feet (15 m)
TIME	Cretaceous period
ANOTHER SPINOSAUR	Baryonyx
SPECIAL FEATURE	Tall sail
FOSSILS FOUND	Egypt, Morocco, Niger

The Spinosaurus lived
95 million years ago.

The first humans appeared
1.6 million years ago.

Triassic Period	Jurassic Period	Cretaceous Period	Tertiary Period
245 Million years ago	208 Million years ago	144 Million years ago	65 Million years ago

Mesozoic Era   Cenozoic Era

29

WEB SITES

To learn more about the Spinosaurus, visit ABDO Publishing Company on the World Wide Web. Web sites about the Spinosaurus are featured on our "Book Links" page. These links are routinely monitored and updated to provide the most current information available.

www.abdopub.com

IMPORTANT WORDS

carnivore a meat-eater.

continent one of the earth's seven main land areas.

Cretaceous period a period of time that happened 144–65 million years ago.

dinosaur a reptile that lived on land 248–65 million years ago.

fossil remains of very old animals and plants commonly found in the ground. A fossil can be a bone, a footprint, or any trace of life.

mammal most living things that belong to this special group have hair, give birth to live babies, and make milk to feed their babies.

paleontologist someone who studies very old life, such as dinosaurs, mostly by studying fossils.

reptiles scaly-skinned animals that cannot make heat inside their bodies.

scavenge to eat animals one did not kill.

tropical weather that is warm and wet.

INDEX